Gr

The Legend of the Little Scottish Dog

BETTY KIRKPATRICK

Crombie Jardine
PUBLISHING LIMITED

Unit 17, 196 Rose Street, Edinburgh EH2 4AT
www.crombiejardine.com

This edition was first published by
Crombie Jardine Publishing Limited in 2005

ISBN 1-905102-04-6

Written by Betty Kirkpatrick
Designed by www.mrstiffy.co.uk
Printed and bound in the United Kingdom by
William Clowes Ltd, Beccles, Suffolk

CONTENTS PAGE

INTRODUCTION

Edinburgh is sometimes referred to as the Athens of the North, a tribute to its many elegant, classical buildings and statues. These statues mostly represent people who have done something to merit historical fame of some kind, but the city's most famous statue is not of one of these: it is of a dog.

The dog in question is Greyfriars Bobby, the first part of his name being a reference to the place with which he was long associated in life: Greyfriars Kirkyard.

Kirk is the Scots word for church and kirkyard is the name given to the burial ground next to a church. This particular kirk and kirkyard take their name from the fact that they are located where a Franciscan friary once stood, monks of the

Franciscan order being known as grey friars from the colour of their habit.

Bobby was a terrier, a member of a breed small in stature but noted for tenacity and courage out of all proportion to such a build. However, it is not for these virtues that Bobby has been honoured with a statue, although, allegedly, he had them in abundance.

It is for his loyalty to his owner for which he is remembered.

This loyalty is all the more impressive because for most of Bobby's life it was unrequited, the owner being dead and buried in Greyfriars Kirkyard long before Bobby went to the great kennel in the sky. When he was alive, Bobby supposedly took up a more or less constant vigil at his master's grave.

Now his statue stands guard opposite the gates to the graveyard and is one of Edinburgh's most visited tourist sites.

BOBBY'S STORY

A great many people, both within Scotland and beyond, have learned at least the bare bones of the story of Greyfriars Bobby. Children are particularly drawn to the tale, partly because of the sheer pathos of it, and partly because most children have a natural liking for dogs.

Thus, it is well known that Bobby was the constant companion of a man who was living in Edinburgh at the time of his death. Naturally, the dog was mystified and bewildered by the whole experience, but he stayed close to the grave, assuming at first that his beloved master would soon wake up. Even after it became clear that this was not going to happen, Bobby remained by the grave, defying all attempts to get him to leave. His master was there and there Bobby, too, was determined to remain, come rain, hail or snow.

But even the most loyal dogs have to eat and there was not much in the vicinity of his master's grave to tempt a terrier's appetite. Then Bobby hit upon a solution to the food problem: he decided to seek a midday meal at the place where his master had usually eaten. If it had been good enough for his master, then it was certainly good enough for him.

Fortunately, the owner of the eating-house recognized Bobby and happily tended to his needs. Bobby became one of his most devoted regulars, but after his meal (and, in winter, after a short rest by the fire), he would be up and away back to the graveyard.

Strictly speaking, he was not meant to be in the graveyard, but many a blind eye was turned as he was left to his vigil. Eventually the owner of the eating-house was called upon to pay a licence fee for Bobby, the local powers-that-be having urged a crackdown on the number of stray dogs roaming the streets of Edinburgh. The licence fee was very high, but the restauranteur could well have afforded it. However, he refused on the grounds that Bobby did not actually belong to him. Indeed, Bobby refused to belong to anyone on this earth.

By now Bobby's story was quite well-known to some of his Edinburgh contemporaries and it was the most mighty of these who came to his aid and saved him from a fate worse than death at the hands of the dog-catchers. No less a personage than the Lord Provost took up the dog's cause, undertaking to pay for Bobby's licence and presenting the dog with a collar. No dog-catcher would dare meddle with the terrier now.

After this encounter with the great of the land, Bobby returned to life in the graveyard until his death in January 1872, by which time he had outlived his master by 14 years. But his loyalty and constancy had never wavered. No wonder some people prefer their dogs to their friends or family!

FACT, NOT FICTION

Several people have written about this popular dog and various details and embellishments have been added, many from imagination or speculation.

However, it is important to remember that the story of Bobby is not a legend. He was a real dog who became the loyal companion of his master, John Gray, probably around 1856.

There are on record reports from people who say that they remember seeing him when they were children, and several of these reports appeared in *The Scotsman* newspaper, published in Edinburgh. When Bobby died in January 1872, having reached the age of sixteen, the paper carried an announcement of his death. He must have been real, to have been declared, so very publicly, dead.

THE ATKINSON VERSION

That so many people know the story of Bobby can be put down, whether directly or indirectly, to one woman. Surprisingly, you might think, she was not a Scot, but an American: one Eleanor Atkinson, née Stackhouse, from Indiana, who had been both a teacher and a newspaper reporter in Chicago before turning her pen to the exploits of Bobby.

Even more surprisingly, Eleanor Atkinson was an American who had never set foot in Edinburgh, despite the fact that her book is liberally sprinkled with quite detailed descriptions of the city from architectural, historical and social perspectives.

In her efforts to make her story as authentic as possible she even went as far as writing much of the dialogue in a version of the Scots language.

Her book *Greyfriars Bobby* was published in 1912, it being originally, it is claimed, written for adults. Of course, although it contains the facts about Bobby, it relies, too, on the creative powers of the author. There is more than a touch of Brigadoon about some of it, together with a liberal splash

of purple prose and a good deal of the kind of schmaltzy sentimentality much loved by the Victorians. In addition, Atkinson sometimes pauses for some high-minded, if over-the-top, philosophical comment, as in 'But ah! in the highest type of man and dog, self-sacrifice, and not self-preservation, is the first law.' Despite all this, the story is of the rattling-good-read variety, if you focus determinedly on the plot.

LOCATION

Atkinson takes advantage of the Scottish countryside as well as the city of Edinburgh when

setting the story. This gives her ample scope for her pen to dwell not only on the filth, starvation and desperation of life in city tenements but also on the beauty of the Scottish countryside and

the joys, and otherwise, of rural life. In fact, although the author could not have known it at the time, this country/city setting was an act of great astuteness on her part, because it became an important feature of the Walt Disney film, based on her book and released in 1961.

OUR HERO

Bobby, most of us will know, was a small dog and those with some slight knowledge of canine matters may even know that he was a terrier. Atkinson adds the information that he was a Skye terrier, a breed with a long coat originating in the Isle of Skye in Scotland. Other writers seem to agree with this, although one adds that Bobby may have had a bit of mongrel strain in him, just to toughen him up a bit. Certainly he was to need all the toughness that he could muster.

The author comes up with rather a romantic reason for Bobby's name. According to Atkinson, the farmer who had employed Auld Jock tells John Traill (the owner

of a restaurant near Greyfriars Kirkyard) how a lady took a fancy to Bobby and, having paid for him, set him up beside her on her cart.

But Bobby was certainly not going to be a lady's pet. As he leapt from the cart and took off down the road, the lady remarked that he should be called Bobby, saying that he was leaving the plough behind and was off

to make his fame and fortune in Edinburgh.

At the time the farmer did not understand the allusion and was enlightened only when Traill explained that the lady was suggesting that the run-away dog should be named after Robert Burns, who had left behind a farm to seek his fortune as a poet in Edinburgh. It is hardly surprising that the farmer did not

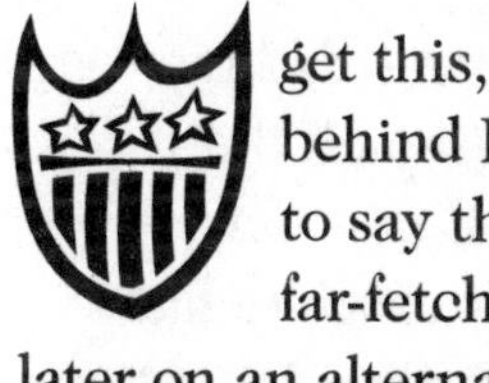

get this, Atkinson's story behind Bobby's name is, to say the least, a little far-fetched. We will see later on an alternative suggestion made by another writer that Bobby was so called from an informal name for a policeman.

However, there is no reason why there should be any great mystery behind Bobby's name at all. Bobby is a common abbreviation for Robert – a very popular Scottish name.

The story of Bobby as told by Atkinson is pretty much the bare-bones version that most of us know, except that she has drawn on her writer's imagination and introduced other characters and adventures and she has, as we have seen, made copious references to social and historical matters that are not strictly relevant to the tale.

Thus, her book tells us that, when Bobby's master died, Bobby refused to forsake the grave, leaving it only to eat at the same place as his master had done when he was alive. The signal for his short journey from graveyard

to restaurant was, in Atkinson's book, the firing of the one o'clock gun that still takes place in Edinburgh and frightens many unwary tourists out of their wits.

The book goes on to tell us how Bobby's place by his dead master's side was assured when he gained the protection of the Lord Provost, who became his licence holder. He had various adventures along the way, some of which are yet to be related here, before dying at quite a ripe old age for a terrier.

BOBBY'S MASTER

In Atkinson's version of Bobby's story, the dog's master, Auld Jock, was really an adopted master, the real owner being Auld Jock's employer. When Jock died, it was discovered from the inscription in his bible that his more formal name was John Gray. Atkinson describes him as being a shepherd in his mid-sixties, who used to attend the Edinburgh weekly market, and who eventually came to the city looking for cheap lodging, when he was paid

off by the farm owner for the winter. This description was later challenged by at least two people who felt that, sitting far away in Chicago, Atkinson had got hold of the wrong John Gray. Their views are aired later in this book.

In Atkinson's story, Bobby's master died in Edinburgh of pneumonia and exhausted old age.

Obviously, he was far from being well off, but he had brought with him to Edinburgh his life savings and this was enough to bury him and save him from a pauper's grave.

Greyfriars Kirkyard was the nearest graveyard to the Cowgate, the poverty-stricken area of Edinburgh where he died.

THE SUPPORTING CAST

In the basic version of Bobby's story there are few characters. Apart from the two protagonists, Bobby and Auld Jock, described already, the supporting cast basically consists of an unnamed eating-house owner and the Lord Provost of Edinburgh. This is certainly not enough for Atkinson who introduces, if not quite a cast of thousands, certainly a goodly number of people who wander in and out of Bobby's life, most of them offering a helping hand.

THE FARMER

The farmer may not seem a very important character and, in truth, Atkinson does not even tell us his name. However, he can be seen as the villain of the piece, since he was, in a sense, the ultimate cause of Bobby's woes. He was the employer of Auld Jock who laid off the shepherd for the winter season, since he was too old and not fit enough for tough winter work. Then it was he (the farmer) who tried to part Bobby from Auld Jock's grave by taking him back to the farm.

However, Atkinson indicates that he is not all villain by telling us that times were hard for the farmer himself and he could not afford to pay staff who could not work.

Furthermore, he is portrayed as seeming genuinely sorry about Auld Jock's demise and did, in his own way, try to help Bobby.

THE RESTAURANT OWNER

In the version of the tale dimly recollected by most us we are unlikely to remember the name of the restaurant owner, although his role in Bobby's life is a significant one. Atkinson reminds us that his name was John Traill. Other writers confirm this, although, as you will find out later in the book, at least one disputes that Traill ever knew Bobby's owner, since he did not take over the restaurant until a considerable time after the death of Auld Jock.

In the Atkinson version, Traill is no stranger to Auld Jock who, she says, regularly attended Traill's establishment (situated near Greyfriars Kirkyard) when he visited the Edinburgh market.

Incidentally, Atkinson describes the establishment as 'a snug little restaurant that was patronized chiefly by the decent poor.' Where the indecent poor went for their refreshment we are not told!

After the death of Bobby's master, Traill, according to Atkinson, did his best for Bobby. Having failed to persuade the dog to make his home with him, he provided food and shelter for him whenever he sought it.

If Traill refused to pay the astonishingly high licence fee of seven shillings demanded by the authorities from dog-owners, it appears that this refusal was made

on the grounds of principle rather than from meanness. He was not the dog's owner.

He did however, Atkinson tells us, go to a great deal of trouble to contact the Lord Provost and enlist his help to save Bobby and enable him to continue his life of unswerving loyalty. Earlier, Atkinson informs us, Traill had intervened on Bobby's behalf with the people who were in charge of the graveyard to allow the dog to stay by his master's remains.

KIRKYARD TENDERS

Some of Atkinson's cast are delegated to look after the graveyard at the centre of the tale. The most important of these is James Brown, who initially was none too pleased to find a dog breaking the law by being within the confines of Greyfriars Kirkyard and threw him out. In time, however, he overcame his fear of the church authorities and turned a blind eye to Bobby's presence by his master's grave. Indeed, he became one of Bobby's

most fervent admirers and, with the assistance of his wife, helped to keep him healthy and well-cared for by giving him the occasional evening meal and making himself responsible for the dog's grooming.

YOUNG PEOPLE IN BOBBY'S LIFE

'Never work with animals and children' is a well-known piece of advice often given to actors. Pity the cast in Atkinson's story, then! Not only did they have to contend with the heart-tugging appeal of the canine central character, but they also had to jockey for importance against a number of children, mostly originating in the poverty-stricken, disease-ridden tenements of Edinburgh. By the time Atkinson was writing *Greyfriars Bobby*, Queen Victoria

was dead, but the author's writing puts her very much in the Victorian tradition. The Victorians just loved a sentimental, heart-wrenching tale of poor and crippled children, as long as such children did not become an actuality and require attention or money.

Topping the heart-tugging personae comes the positively Dickensian character, Tommy Barr, a crippled boy who got around as best he could with the aid of some extempore crutches made by his father from wood retrieved from the back of an old chair.

It was Tommy who, having spotted the hapless Bobby trying unsuccessfully to get out of the locked Greyfriars gates in order to reach his source of food, sought the assistance of a more mobile friend to help Bobby make the transition from graveyard to restaurant.

This friend may have been more able-bodied, but she was no less

poverty-stricken than Tommy. Her name was Ailie Lindsey, later in young adulthood to become a waitress in the Traill restaurant, and she was able to assist in Bobby's search for sustenance only with the help of her grandmother's shoes. Otherwise, she would have had to take the painful, and non-respectable, option of going barefoot.

The culmination of Ailie's and Tommy's contribution to Bobby's welfare occurred when they rounded up the ragged children of the neighbourhood to collect money for Bobby's dog licence, not realizing that the Lord Provost was going to pay for this.

This seemed an impossible task, given the poverty of the neighbourhood, but this is fiction and in fiction all things are possible. With the help of a student called Geordie Ross, the urchins met the seemingly unachievable target of seven shillings.

Ailie and Tommy are joined in the young cast of the story by some boys from George Heriot's School, then a charity school known as George Heriot's Hospital, located near Greyfriars churchyard. Most of these boys remain anonymous, but we are introduced to Geordie Ross and Sandy Macgregor. These two stalwarts, with their

schoolmates and Bobby, were involved in many schoolboy pranks and adventures but, on leaving school, fulfilled the Victorian ideal of poor boy makes good by becoming respectively a medical student and a clerk in the publishing house of W&R Chambers.

Fortunately, in these positions they were still able to help

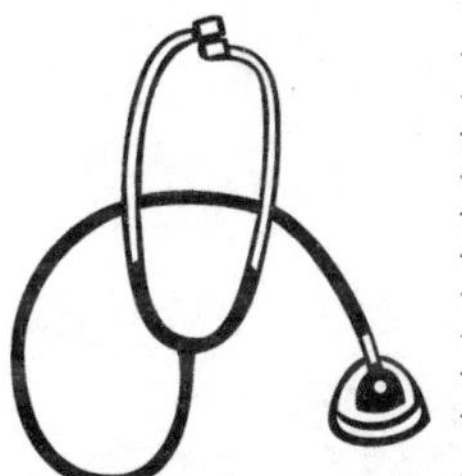

Bobby - Sandy helping Traill to locate the Lord Provost to ask help for Bobby and Geordie using his medical skills to help Bobby recover from nasty injuries sustained while rolling down the rock of Edinburgh Castle. As we have already seen, Geordie was also able to help the neighbourhood children in their collection for Bobby's licence fee.

THE LORD PROVOST

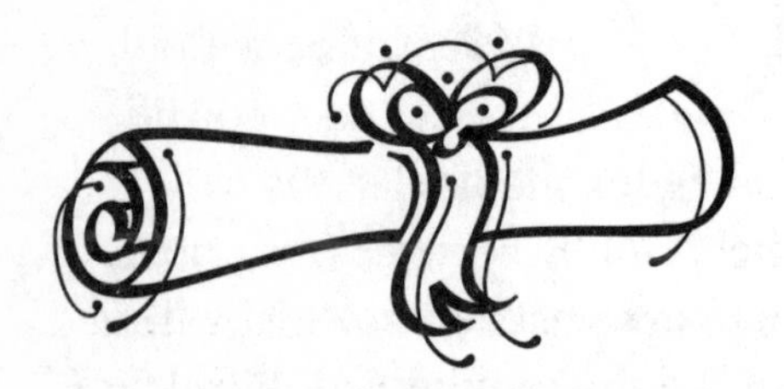

You may think that such an august person should have come further up the cast list of Atkinson's doggy tale, but chronologically he fits in here. The Lord Provost of the day was Sir William Chambers who, with his brother Robert, was one of the founders of the publishing firm of W&R Chambers and, as such, was the employer of Bobby's friend Sandy Macgregor, whom we met in the previous section.

Sir William Chambers played an important role in the history of Edinburgh, and, indeed, he played an important role in the story of Greyfriars Bobby.

When Traill was made to appear before the magistrates for refusing

to pay a licence for Bobby, on the very reasonable grounds that he was not the dog's owner, Traill sought the intervention of Sir William, who was a known animal lover.

Having been told the story of Bobby, Sir William paid the licence fee himself and presented a collar to Bobby with an inscription that testified to this—'Greyfriars Bobby from the Lord Provost 1867, licensed'.

In the Atkinson version of the tale, the presentation of the collar took place in another famous part of Edinburgh's history, St Giles Cathedral, and it was enthusiastically witnessed by the

crowd of tenement urchins who had valiantly collected enough money to pay for Bobby's licence, unaware of the Lord Provost's involvement.

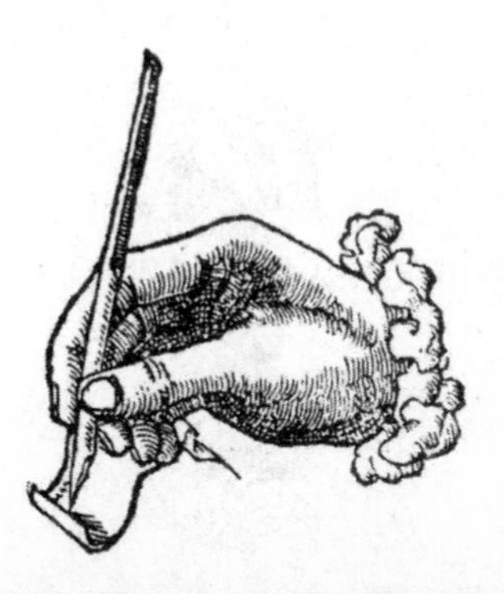

SERGEANT SCOTT AND THE MILITARY CONNECTION

Apart from the statue of Greyfriars Bobby, Edinburgh's other great tourist attraction is the castle. These two attractions were linked, according to Atkinson, when Bobby got involved with the soldiers there and made a friend, one Sergeant Scott.

Several times in the course of her book the author mentions that Bobby was a lover of music and liked to perform antics in time to it. It was this love of music,

particularly the skirl of the pipes, that made Bobby follow the soldiers on their route march.

Atkinson has the little dog following the soldiers to the farm where he once lived with his master. He was happy enough to spend some time there and even to be petted for a while by the little girl, Elsie, the daughter of the farmer. However, Bobby had no intention of taking up permanent

residence there. According to Atkinson, the farmer had tried to make Bobby do just that when Auld Jock died, but Bobby was having none of it then and he was having none of it now. With difficulty he escaped Elsie's loving clutches, and set off in hot pursuit of the soldiers.

Bobby happily followed them back to the castle esplanade, but this did not prove to be altogether a happy experience for the dog. He must have enjoyed being admired and petted by the soldiers such as Sergeant Scott, who took a particular interest in him.

However, Bobby came up against a difficult problem when the time came for him to go back to the graveyard and take up his vigil. The castle gates were locked and an offer by the sergeant to take Bobby back to Greyfriars Kirkyard was refused by his commanding officer. A thick fog had come down and walking in the city would be dangerous.

However, Bobby was not a dog to let a few locked gates or a bit of fog keep him from his duty and, according to Atkinson, he set about returning to Greyfriars via the steep and rugged face

of the castle rock. This descent involved scrabbling, rolling and falling, leading not only to exhaustion but to bad bruises and injuries. Fortunately, Geordie Ross, introduced previously, in the cast of young people, was able to treat Bobby, but the terrier had paid very dearly for his romp with the soldiers, although he and the sergeant remained friends. Atkinson relates how Traill persuaded Scott to buy Bobby some steak once a month as a

doggy treat. The local children must have envied him.

THE FILM

Eleanor Atkinson's story of Bobby's life was just asking to be made into a film and Walt Disney duly obliged. The great man even made a trip to Edinburgh to view Bobby's stomping-ground. The original idea had been to use the beautiful city of Edinburgh as a backdrop for the film version of Bobby, but it was felt that there were too many modern buildings and that anachronisms such as telegraph poles would get in the way.

Therefore, much of the 'Edinburgh' setting for the film was a fabricated set made in the Shepperton Studios in Middlesex.

The country scenes were shot at a farm near Gifford, not far from Edinburgh, although some of the buildings had to be temporarily modified in order to conform to the required period.

An eighteen-month-old Skye terrier

who was, by a happy coincidence, also called Bobby in real life, played the part of the inimitable Bobby.

The film, released in 1961, has alternatively been described as heart-tugging or stomach-churning, depending on the attitude of the viewer. In the light of Bobby's continuing popularity, I wonder if we are not due for a revival or a remake.

Who could resist a canine *Braveheart*?

THE MACGREGOR VERSION

In 1990 a book was published entitled *Greyfriars Bobby. The Real Story at Last*. Written by Forbes Macgregor, it challenged some of the facts that had been imparted to us by Atkinson.

POLICEMAN, NOT SHEPHERD

Macgregor claimed that the results of his research in Edinburgh's archives and elsewhere proved that Bobby's master, although he was indeed John Gray and was also known as Auld Jock, was not a shepherd, but a policeman, when he became Bobby's master. Furthermore, he was not a lonely old man, but had a wife and son as companions. Like Atkinson's Auld Jock, Macgregor's John Gray was resident in the country before coming to the city, but he had come to find work. He was a gardener by trade but a very severe winter had made agricultural and horticultural work difficult to come by.

There is a difference in age, too. Macgregor indicates that Bobby's master was forty years old when he came to Edinburgh and applied for the police force,

while Atkinson's description puts Bobby's master in his mid-sixties. The death of Atkinson's character was significantly quicker on stage, as it were, for Macgregor's John Gray was ill for quite some months before he died of tuberculosis in February 1858.

Macgregor tells us that, when he was appointed as a policeman, John Gray was given a policeman's

dwelling near the Cowgate. This was far from being a desirable residential part of the city, poverty, disease and crime being rife, but policemen were required to live in the area of their beats. To help him in his work, John Gray, like the other members of the Edinburgh force, was given a watchdog. From Macgregor's story it appears that Bobby was the policeman's second dog, being acquired by him around 1856.

Today a policeman in uniform accompanied by a terrier for added protection would raise a few laughs, or, at least, a few smothered titters, but then we have become accustomed to the somewhat larger German Shepherd acting as a helpmeet to our enforcers of law and order.

THE RESTAURANT OWNER

The cast of the Macgregor book is not the same as that of Atkinson's, but we can allow for a little poetic licence either way.

It is worth mentioning, however, that John Traill, who is such a powerful figure in the story, does not enter the Macgregor version until 1862, more than four years after John Gray's death.

THE NAME GAME

The reason given by Atkinson for our hero's name is, not unexpectedly, called into question by this book. Here Macgregor tells us that John Gray's son, who was known, somewhat predictably, as Young Jock, gave Bobby his name. Since the Skye terrier awaiting a name was to be a policeman's dog, and since policemen were known informally as bobbies, (a reference to the abbreviated version of the name of the police force's

founder, Sir Robert Peel), Young Jock christened the new family member Bobby. Such ingenuity!

THE LUNCH-TIME GUN

In Atkinson's version of Bobby's story the little dog knew it was time to seek sustenance at his local eating-house, even when his master was alive, when the one o'clock gun boomed out from Edinburgh Castle.

Not so, according to Macgregor. In his version it was Sergeant Scott, whom we have already met in the Atkinson version and who plays a slightly bigger role in Bobby's life here, who taught the dog the significance of the gun.

In any case, Macgregor reminds us that this cannon, fired at one o'clock exactly so that all citizens of Edinburgh might know the time and adjust their timepieces accordingly, was not set up until June 1861, by which time John Gray had been dead for several years.

THE GILHOOLEY VERSION

James Gilhooley, an engineer who embarked on the task of researching Bobby's story, challenged both the Atkinson and the Macgregor versions in 1999.

Just to confuse us, he claims that his research has brought to light yet another John Gray.

The name is beginning to make John Smith seem positively rare by comparison!

ENTER ANOTHER JOHN GRAY

Gilhhooley's John Gray apparently died within a few days of Macgregor's John Gray – hence the confusion.

This third bearer of the name was neither shepherd, nor policeman, but a farmer from the Borders town of Skirling.

But worse is yet to come. According to Gilhooley, the John Gray who was the master of the loyal hound is not buried in

Greyfriars Kirkyard at all, but was laid to rest in a pauper's grave in East Preston Street, some distance away.

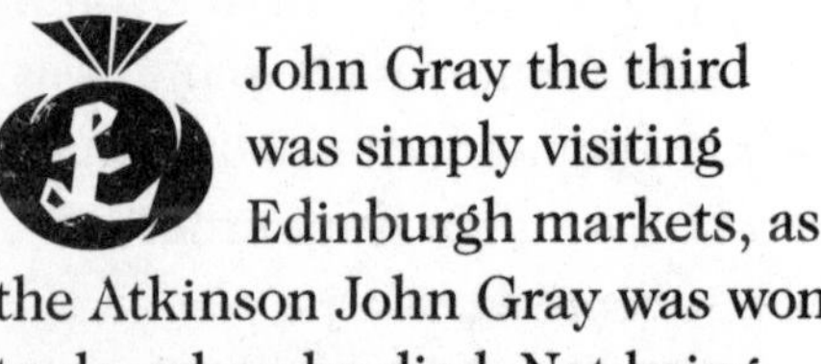

John Gray the third was simply visiting Edinburgh markets, as the Atkinson John Gray was wont to do, when he died. Not being a resident, and not having any money with him, he would not have been allowed to inhabit a grave in Greyfriars.

Gilhhooley's account has Bobby remaining in the area of Greyfriars after his master's death. This, apparently, was partly because his master rented a room in nearby Bristo place when he came to the market, and so Bobby was acquainted with the area. But it was partly because he was receiving sustenance at the hands of a kindly local pieshop owner. Poor Bobby! This is not nearly so romantic a tale!

So much controversy in
what started out as an idyll!
Nevermind! Facts are undeniably
very important in life, but let us
not them allow them to spoil the
story of our loyal canine hero. His
is a story more rooted in emotion.

BOBBY'S AFTERLIFE

So overcome with emotion on hearing Bobby's story, a lady called Baroness Angela Georgina Burdett-Coutts offered to erect a memorial fountain as a monument to him. Being a noted animal lover, she was concerned that animals as well as humans would benefit from this. Thus the monument, unveiled in November 1873, consisted of a drinking fountain with an animal trough below, the whole topped by a

splendid bronze statue of Bobby created by the famous sculptor, William Brodie.

Bobby's life was far from being incident-free and that of his statue followed suit. The memorial has not been a fountain for some considerable time. It was removed in 1965, although the water supply had been cut off some years before that. Sadly, the fountain had begun to be used as a

receptacle for rubbish by passers-by. Oh, the indignity of it!

Fortunately, the statue received a facelift in the late 1980s but, by then, several misadventures had taken place. It had been vandalized in the mid 1950s, stolen as a student prank in 1963, knocked off its perch by a butcher's van in 1971, covered in yellow paint in 1979 and dislodged in a traffic accident in 1986.

The life of the statue of Bobby has clearly not been an easy one.

Concern was voiced for both the safety of the statue and of the admirers who went out into the middle of the road in order to photograph it. In the early 1980s permission was asked to move it to the safer territory of the graveyard, but this was refused.

Meanwhile, in 1981, the Dog Aid Society of Scotland had paid for the erection of a memorial to Bobby to be placed within the confines of Greyfriars. This memorial, which bears the inscription 'Let his Loyalty and Devotion be a Lesson to us all', does not stand on consecrated ground, but on a triangular plot of grass in front of Greyfriars Kirk, where it is thought Bobby was buried. Being a dog, he was not allowed to have a resting place near his master in the actual

graveyard, despite his intense loyalty.

This memorial to Bobby, laid by a royal personage in the shape of the Duke of Gloucester, is made of red granite, as is the gravestone marking the grave of John Gray. This was the Atkinson John Gray, for it was paid for by American fans of Bobby who had grown to love the dog through the pages of her book, and who remembered him in the inscription on the memorial to his master.

John Gray

Died 1858

'Auld Jock'

Master of 'Greyfriars Bobby'

'And Even In His Ashes

Most Beloved'

Erected By

American lovers of Bobby

I will not even attempt to follow this.

INDEX

Crombie Jardine
PUBLISHING LIMITED

Unit 17, 196 Rose Street, Edinburgh EH2 4AT
www.crombiejardine.com

Crombie Jardine books are available from

Bookpost

P.O.Box 29

Douglas

Isle of Man

IM99 1BQ

Tel: 01624 677237

Fax: 01624 670923

Email: bookshop@enterprise.net

NESSIE

The Legend of the Loch Ness Monster

105x85mm, 128pp, pb, £2.99

ISBN 1-905102-05-4

SCOTTISH WIT & WISDOM

The Meanings Behind
Famous Scottish Sayings

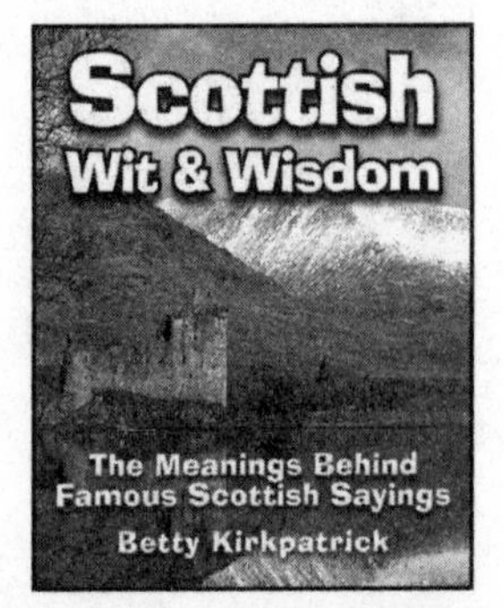

105x85mm, £2.99, 128pp, pb

ISBN 1-905102-07-0

AULD SCOTTISH GRANNIES' REMEDIES

A Haggis a Day Keeps the Doctor Away

105x85mm, 128pp, pb, £2.99

ISBN 1-905102-06-2